# Teaching on Poverty Rock

Joby McGowan

PublishAmerica
Baltimore

© 2004 by Joby McGowan.
All rights reserved. No part of this book may be reproduced, stored in a retrieval system or transmitted in any form or by any means without the prior written permission of the publishers, except by a reviewer who may quote brief passages in a review to be printed in a newspaper, magazine or journal.

First printing

ISBN: 1-4137-1455-2
PUBLISHED BY PUBLISHAMERICA, LLLP
www.publishamerica.com
Baltimore

Printed in the United States of America

# FOREWORD

This is the true portrayal of how I saw my first year teaching on Mercer Island. All of the names of those involved, aside from my own, have been changed. This story reflects my point of view. No doubt, this story would reflect a different point of view if retold by any other person included in this work.

# APRIL 2002

My resume looked magnificent. At the very least, I looked flawless on paper. I would hire myself, given the opportunity. I sent out at least thirty-two resumes to both public and private schools in the greater Seattle metropolitan area. Every packet included my Washington state teaching credentials and a wad of letters of recommendation from previous administrators, colleagues I had taught with, and parents of youngsters I had guided, or more honestly miss-guided, down the first grade and Kindergarten years of elementary school. Now it was time to wait for some lucky school to snap me up. So, I waited.

# MAY 2002

Somewhere along the line in time when teaching becomes more challenging, near the end of the school year, I received an e-mail from Michelle in the Human Resources Department of one of Seattle's most prestigious schools located on Mercer Island. If I would have had the foresight to know what that one click of opening her e-mail would bring I might have been just as well to dump that e-mail in the trash. Since I didn't know anything, I charged ahead, as I do blindly with most things in my life, and read the e-mail.

"Dear Mr. McGowan, We would like to offer you an opportunity to interview for elementary teaching positions for the 2002-2003 academic year."

The e-mail went on with the particulars about dates and times. In conclusion she urged me to e-mail or call the HR office to make arrangements if I was so inclined. I just so happened to be inclined. I clicked reply and expressed an interest in being considered to lead a flock of youngsters for one year down the academic road. I asked Michelle if it were at all possible to conduct a preliminary phone interview. Other schools that had contacted me from the greater Seattle area had all agreed to this request. If after that time there was still a mutual interest I would be happy to make the trip out to Seattle for an in-person visit. Well, wouldn't you know it? The interview team felt it would be best if we met in person from the get go so as to "better understand one another." For those of you who haven't worked in an educational setting before the translation on all that jargon really means, "Bring your ass out here so we can size each other up in person." So, feverishly I searched online to find a reasonable airfare to dash off to Seattle's Mercer Island.

Mercer Island, Washington rests in the middle of Lake Washington just east to the city of Seattle. The floating Interstate 90 bridge connects Mercer Island with downtown Seattle. It is one of Seattle's most distinguished communities. Elitism is at its highest on Mercer Island. Those who go without have no place on Mercer Island.

I boarded a jet and took off for Seattle. Upon arriving I was interviewed at the administrative office. There was a panel of five people on the interview committee. A significant amount of time was spent asking and answering questions about how to handle specific situations involving parents with un-realistic demands. The rest of the time focused on teaching practices. Julie, an administrator on the interview team, pulled me aside as I left from the interview an hour later to let me know that I was a strong candidate and asked that I be sure to let her know if another offer comes my way before this panel made a decision. I explained that I already had an offer from a school in West Seattle. Julie

8

asked if I could wait to render a decision for the competing school until Tuesday of the following week. I agreed.

As I jetted back to Iowa to wrap up the last few days of school I remembered thinking Seattle would be my new home. I was enthusiastic about this new turn of events.

Tuesday evening of the following week I received a phone call from Julie of the interview team. I was offered a job. She said it was for either a first or second grade position. I said, "OK, I will take first grade." She explained that the placement wouldn't be final until a few weeks down the road. I chalked this up as the first of many misunderstandings I would have with the school.

# JUNE 2002

I was informed via e-mail a few weeks after accepting the teaching position that I would be teaching second grade. Hurray! I hadn't taught second grade before. What the hell, right? A new grade level would only be a challenge and help broaden my horizons.

# AUGUST 2002

I piloted the Ryder truck to my new school on August 1st. I unloaded what seemed like a zillion boxes of school stuff. How in the world did I end up with so much junk? This was the second time I had met Mrs. Lakewood, the principal of my new school. Though she greeted me with warm affection and kindness I still wondered what the hell I had done. I sold my house, left a school I had loved, left friends, family, etc. New adventures. Onward!

A few days later I began to unpack the gazillion boxes of school things in room eleven of my new school. I slapped up all kinds of bulletin boards, organized boxes of crayons, markers, paper, etc. Perhaps one of the most evident things about the school was that I wasn't in need of anything. All of the furniture in my classroom matched. There was an abundance of materials. The storage room of supplies overflowed with a rainbow of colored construction paper, markers, folders, paper, pens, staplers, glue, tape and the list went on.

Late in August the New Teacher Workshop began. "Rah! Rah! Welcome to the best school year ever. You are the meat and potatoes of this work force. Thank you for joining our team." So, with my perma-grin plastered to my face I truly was enthusiastic about the new school year ahead.

We had a zillion technology meetings. All staff members were issued brand new i-Book laptop computers that fall. The school staff met a few days before students arrived to go over procedures and meet the new members of the faculty. I was issued a binder no less than 4 inches thick titled "S.O.P" (Standard Operating Procedures). Great! When the hell was I going to read that thesis? Much time was spent talking about emergency procedures during those first staff meetings before school started. There were to be ten fire drills and ten earthquake drills that year. Ten! Safety was a top priority with our principal, Mrs. Lakewood. We must have every possible scenario mapped out and practiced in the event that a real emergency would threaten our safety. I had trouble deciphering if Mrs. Lakewood was the principal of our elementary school or if she was a police officer hired to enforce the laws of the educational institution. Coming from Iowa I was well versed in procedures for both fire and tornado drills. In Seattle earthquakes were a threat as well. I hadn't read the S.O.P. manual and asked Mrs. Lakewood in one of the early meetings how I would know the difference between earthquake and tornado drills. I asked what signal was used for each emergency? Laughter erupted from the meeting. This was the first of many times that I served as entertainment for my new colleagues. Officer Lakewood directly informed me that tornados are not a threat in Seattle. I should also make sure that I read the S.O.P. manual as soon as possible so I can be up to speed on all the routines. Translation: You are an idiot Joby. I have everything spelled out for you as to how you should be spending every second in every possible situation in the S.O.P. Manual. Any question asked that could be answered by reading the S.O.P. Manual was considered a waste of time in Officer Lakewood's eyes. I knew this by the crook in her lip that appeared after just such a question was asked.

As more supplies were delivered to each classroom we approached the Labor Day weekend. I met my second grade team. Sandy, Teresa, Karen and Deb. Karen and Deb shared one of the classrooms. They each worked two days a week and alternated teaching each Monday. The team of five would lead this year's second graders onward.

# SEPTEMBER 2002

The first day of school rolled in and I put on my best "Happy New School Year Smile". I was struggling to let go of how things were done at my old school. At my "old school" the students drug their supplies to school two days before school ever started over the lunch hour, met the teacher and familiarized themselves with the building. Teachers met their students and families at 9:00 the first day of school on Mercer Island. Who the hell rigged this one-man circus up? How exactly does one person really touch base with every family and child at 9:00 on the first day of school? Usually I have teacup saucer sized sweat circles around the armpits of my shirt by that time on the first day of school. All twenty-three students assigned to my leadership bounced in with a bag of supplies and lunch, or money to buy tickets for lunch. Each child was accompanied by at least one parent. Many came with two. A few drug their nannies in as a stand in for their parent(s). Several mothers wanted to know what time lunch was. Would I call if their child had any trouble today? Where was I from? Did I know that the son of one mother had asthma?

Then I met Mrs. Craston, Mike's mom. She was a tall, pale, blonde haired woman with cat hair sticking out all over her clothes. She butted in front of another parent to ask,

"When will you begin using classroom volunteers?"

"We will go over all of those issues at Parent Information Night next week." Mental note to self: Craston had the potential to be a crazy one.

It took all of three minutes to determine I was up against a monster. I was under the impression that second grade was the "Cadillac" of all grades in the elementary school. Many second grade teachers had told me this in the past. It appeared not to be true. It was an unruly bunch that first morning. After I finally ushered the very last mother, father, nanny and grandparent from room eleven I closed the door and drew the blind covering the window leading to the hallway. I turned around and saw four of the twenty-three students reading the piles of books I had left on the tables for the first day entrance activity. Nineteen of the students were walking around the room touching base with old pals from last year, examining everything in sight. I dug deep in my pockets for one of those magic transition activities I had learned in college. I clapped my big hands together and began singing a made up song about it being time to freeze, listen, and be ready to learn. Well, as I sung, few showed any interest. Welcome to your new school. It was home of the "We do what we feel like it, when we feel like it" student population. This was going to be harder than I had imagined.

All through the first day of school I wondered how I was going to gain some control with these kids without losing my sanity? I had never in my short six years of teaching ever had a class that did not at least listen to me when I spoke and who didn't at least follow the directions the first few days of school.

Immediately after the first recess at 10:50 the twenty-three second graders bounced into the room and started digging into their bags. I was instantly irritated because it looked like there was a group effort to take over the room.

"What are you all doing?"

"This is snack time, Mr. McGowan."

"Ahh, No it isn't. Put your snacks away. Who said it was snack time? We will have a snack this afternoon."

We did. Some of the kids brought an elaborate snack including a juice bottle, half a sandwich, some crackers and a cookie. There were a few students with sushi. Snack was more like the boxed lunches I had eaten on recent flights.

New rule: Only one snack item, or what you can eat in ten minutes. We are not having a smorgasbord in second grade.

The first day was long. I missed my old school.

# DAY TWO OF SCHOOL

It was similar to the first. I spent a lot of time wondering what magic I could cook up on my fifteen minute recess and thirty minute lunch breaks to help bring order to our classroom, or at the very least some responsibility to the students to listen and follow directions. Second grade was not the "Cadillac".

At 3:45 that afternoon a tall figure appeared in my door. It was cat haired Mrs. Craston. She gripped a paper with some scrawl on it in one of her claws. I invited her to sit down. She began right away with

"You yell too much. Have you ever tried positive re-enforcement? What is this I hear about the kids only being able to have one snack? Don't you know that snack is supposed to be in the morning? It is a school wide rule. It isn't fair to the kids that you put the restriction of one snack on them as well as move snack time to the afternoon. You may have been successful in Iowa, at your old school, but this is how "we" do things here."

First off, who the hell are "we"? Was Mrs. Craston a school employee? Or, was this the infamous "we" that is often made up of parents who want to be the "we" that run a school? It was the later. She went on.

"When will you be contacting people about volunteer opportunities? All the teachers use them, you know?"

She would also need a copy of the e-mail addresses of all the parents that I collected on the first day of school so she could send out e-mails to them to inform the families about the class parties and room events, etc."

Well, we were off to a stellar start. She barely took a breath between each question and demand. She finally stopped. My only reaction was the following,

"It sounds like you are very unhappy with this placement for your son, Mike. Let's go talk to Mrs. Lakewood and look into an alternate placement for him this year."

"Absolutely not. He can't be moved. It wouldn't work." she spat back.

I asked Mrs. Craston for some space and said,

"You are the most abrasive person I have every worked with. I am not up for a whole year of these attacks."

She looked dumbfounded. I think it was another unwritten rule on Mercer Island that the teachers did not ever stand up for themselves against the patrons. I began to see that it was the expectation for teachers to make every accommodation possible to make sure parents were pleased with the program in the classroom.

I already hated Mercer Island. I hated Mrs. Craston too. It was only the second day of school. 178 days to go.

I began to receive the following notes and e-mails…

"Mr. McGowan, Every Tuesday after school I will pick Samantha up at car pick up. She has dance class."

"Hi. Mr. McGowan, Lisa has soccer practice every Friday after school. Please help her to remember not to get on the bus and to get changed into her soccer outfit for practice on Fridays."

"Dear Joby, I just wanted to let you know that Joshua will be on bus route number 413 on Tuesday, Wednesday and Thursday of each week. Beginning tomorrow he will start defense training. He is very excited."

What the hell is defense training? Come to find out it was some sort of martial arts program. It was just what we needed, a seven year old who was capable of kicking all of our asses.

After a dozen or so of these letters and e-mails poured in from many different families I had to ask myself, "Do I look like a receptionist?" I needed a spreadsheet to keep track of which child did what on which night of the week. I could devote the entire back bulletin board to organizing the schedule for each child. I barely remember my own appointments and commitments. How was I going to remember that of twenty-three second graders?

We bounded through the next week of school and I prepared for Curriculum Night. Curriculum Night is the school-designated evening for parents to come and mow you over with questions about the academic program in your classroom.

In an effort to take the pressure off of myself, I had learned from a friend, who taught Kindergarten for many years, that I could engage the parents in several of the activities that the kids do during the day as the Curriculum Night presentation. This was in lieu of standing in front of the parents and delivering all the information in a lecture format. This may help them see what their kids do on a daily basis. You can talk while they work highlighting the benefits and how you would meet the needs of struggling and gifted students for each activity. So, this is what I did. It was a grand time. I enjoyed it. Many parents laughed and enjoyed it too.

As I drew the circus of Curriculum Night to a close I spoke with Darrin's mom, Mrs. Ashton. She informed me that she was one of the room parents along with Samantha's mom and, you guessed it, none other than Mrs. Craston. If I would have known then what I know now I would have told Mrs. Ashton, "Thanks for the heads up. That Craston woman is crazy. Isn't she?" I didn't. I thanked her and told her I looked forward to working with her.

I turned around and ran into Mrs. Craston. Her face was pinched. Her eyes darted back and forth as she spoke.

"You didn't talk about volunteers. When and how are you going to use volunteers this year?"

Well, throwing on my best professional look, I explained that I would use them on an as needed basis that year. When events or situations came up that merited help I would ask for it. There were also six volunteer opportunities to sign up for on the front table, which I, by divine intervention, did remember to tell parents about before they left. They included things such as field trip chaperoning, party coordinators, people to donate supplies, etc. She raced over and signed up for all of them after informing me that the way "we" use volunteers on Mercer Island is to have parents in the classroom on a rotating weekly basis. Translation: You are doing it wrong, Joby.

I erased the white board, drew the blinds, and gathered my

things to go home that evening. Officer Lakewood walked into room eleven and asked me how Curriculum Night went. I chirped a line about how nice it was and how I enjoyed meeting the parents. She went on.

"Mrs. Craston stopped me and said you aren't using any volunteers this year. Perhaps you can figure out a way to make it work for her."

Between the time Mrs. Craston left room eleven and got to the front door she had drug dog sniffed out the principal, Mrs. Lakewood, to let her know how bad I was and that I wasn't going to use volunteers and that something needed to be done. I looked in the dictionary when I got home that night. Craston's picture wasn't under the word "crazy". I penciled it in my own edition of Webster's on her behalf.

# SECOND WEEK OF SCHOOL

I began to receive a few e-mails and voice mail messages about homework. On Mercer Island "we" give homework packets each week. "We" do not send individual nightly assignments for kids. Hold the phone! What are "we" doing giving second graders nightly homework? Baffled by this newest addition to the long list of "must dos" outlined in the S.O.P. Manual, which I still hadn't read, I went to my team to get more information.

Sure enough, thirty to forty-five minutes of homework each evening was a requirement in second grade. I dug around through old files and found some worksheets. I cooked up a few writing prompts and created a form for students to use each evening to record the number of minutes they read from a book of their choice. Satisfied with my work, though requiring thirty to forty-five minutes of homework each night for these kids was completely against everything I knew to be developmentally appropriate, I whipped up the packets and sent them home the third week of school. Case closed.

At the second staff meeting of the year the librarian, Mrs. Keptog, stood up and said she wanted to thank Mr. McGowan for instituting a new procedure. She went on to explain to the staff that anytime you wanted library time for your class, all you needed to do was to send your kids up to the media center. Joby had been sending a handful of kids throughout the day over the course of the first few days of school. Mrs. Keptog had spunk. I admired her light-hearted approach from the first time I talked with her. She was eccentric and in tune to the wants of young children. She was a magnet that drew people to her through her entertaining story telling and hilarious sense of humor. The staff erupted in a sea of laughter. The feeling was light as we all enjoyed my mishap. I didn't realize that students had only one opportunity per week to check out books. The said check out time was during their scheduled library period. Of course all of this was outlined in the S.O.P. manual. I explained to the staff that at my "old school" we were allowed to send kids to the library anytime during the day to return books and check out new ones. In talking with Mrs. Keptog later she explained which forces were restricting her from allowing the open door policy in the media center. Officer Lakewood looked at me and said,

"You can only get by on the excuse of how things were done at your old school for so long."

Translation: We do it differently here. Read your S.O.P. manual and figure this stuff out soon.

I received an e-mail from Kevin's mom. "Joby, Thanks for you e-mails and updates from room eleven. Jake (Kevin's dad) and I enjoyed Curriculum Night. We have been practicing the "TA DA DA DA" song and dance at home! (I taught the kids and parents a song and dance called the Tootie Ta) Kevin really likes your class. He sometimes has had difficulty with transitions, but this one seems, at least to us, to have been very easy for him. Kevin is very excited to have a male teacher. I think that your creativity in teaching the materials through interesting games and presentations has really held his interest. Please let us know if there is anything we can do to help you in the class. Thanks for your energy and positive approach with the children!"

I sucked every possible breath I could out of her e-mail. Oxygen in full doses like that was hard to come by on Mercer Island. Kevin and his family were climbing the ladder steps to be number one with me.

The e-mail and voicemail messages continued. They had common threads in them such as "You are not giving enough homework! The spelling words are too easy! There are no challenging assignments in the homework packets! We need more homework!" Eve's dad told me that I should really be giving the kids an hour or more of homework each night. He remembered having lots of homework as a student and wanted his children to have the same experience. Ummm, Yah, that was when he was in college, not second grade. You have probably already wondered what Mrs. Craston had to say about the homework. Well, she concurred that it wasn't enough and that it was too easy. I wasn't providing a challenge for her son, Mike. He wouldn't possibly be ready for the workload in third grade without more homework in second grade.

Armed with the continual stream of helpful suggestions for how I should be organizing homework I was in a general state of being pissed off when the subject came up. I gathered every worksheet master book I could find. I knocked on Teresa's door, one of my teaching mates, to borrow any books she had that were copyright free. I must have looked like a half crazed bull as I whirl winded up to the teacher workroom, arms loaded with books. I spent the better part of an evening photocopying a zillion sheets. I began to put together homework packets to last for the next four weeks. Each packet contained no less than thirty-five sheets of homework in addition to the reading requirement of fifteen minutes per evening. I made sure there were challenging assignments which included, but were not limited to, triple digit addition, subtraction and multiplication. We had not talked about multiplication yet, but since I was working with Einstein offspring who desperately needed a challenge I figured they would already know how to do this. I copied Geometry and Geography papers. I threw in things about measurement and time. There were sheets about calculating values of money and the list went on. Satisfied with the four trees I had snuffed out on this ever so important homework in the eyes of some vocal parents, I walked back to room eleven exhausted.

Amy's dad sent an e-mail. "Our school is lucky to have found you, and I think it is great to have some men in the classroom! " Thank you Amy's dad for taking the time to communicate your appreciation. One kind word a day helps keep McGowan out of the nut house.

There is a recognizable Jewish population on Mercer Island. Great by me. I don't care what religion you are. Do what you believe in. I am all for organized religion and the freedom to embrace it. We were fast approaching a Jewish holiday. Guess who's family was Jewish? Mrs. Craston e-mailed me to be sure that I knew that some of the students would be out of school for one day the following week. She went on to explain in great detail that teachers should not plan anything exciting for the days the students who practiced Judaism weren't in attendance. I was already exhausted from the ongoing stream of free suggestions and amount of time she spent telling me what I should and should not do. I wrote back and said that it would be a normal school day like any other. The activities would not be altered because some of the students wouldn't be there. Did this mean that she expected me to plan things of a lower interest for those students who were Methodist, Lutheran or Buddhist because the kids who practiced Judaism were not going to be there for one day? Whatever. Religion is a choice. I was not going to punish or hold back kids, nor the academic program in room eleven, simply because the religion of some students required them to stay home for a day. By all means, stay home. Practice your religious beliefs. I support you in your effort. I do not, however, have to impose restrictions on the rest of the class because a few children were going to be out for one day to practice their religious beliefs. I didn't bother to share any of this with Officer Lakewood.

In an effort to help the kids in room eleven feel good and to have a meaningful reason to use the US postal system I penned each child a letter and sent it to their home. I received an e-mail from Eve's mom a few days later. "Hi Mr. McGowan. Are we still on for tomorrow morning at ten? (Eve's mom was coming to teach an art lesson.) Eve is so excited about it. Thank you so much for the nice letter you send Eve. She read it aloud to everyone and wrote back to you! Thank you for your encouragement and enthusiasm."

No. Thank you, Eve's mom, for making an effort to appreciate me while I sink.

Autumn was a girl assigned to my class. I had heard much about her prior years in school. Apparently there were incidents in the past with aggressive behavior, vocal demands, and physical altercations with adults. It was good information to have. I had not observed anything from her but compliance and follow through on procedures and expectations. Apparently it was time to see otherwise. I had gathered the kids together. They all were having a snack of some sort that they had brought from home. I turned around after selecting a book to read to the kids while they ate. Autumn was standing in front of me. Her teeth were gritted and she said, "I wanna go home."

"Oh? I know how you feel. I want to get out of here too. I will share a snack with you. Take a seat and I will bring you something."

"I wanna go home now!"

"Well, sorry to tell you but going home is not a choice right now."

We tell kids all the time about their "choices". Who was the idiot who thought phrasing expectations in the form of "choices" would be a non-threatening way of doing it? Beats me.

Autumn stomped over to the coat and mailbox area of our room, packed her bag and stood up. She glanced back at me to see if I was aware of her actions. I was. I watched. I sat down on a chair to see what would unfold next. She went to the door and pushed as hard as she could to get the push bar to go in so the door would open. It didn't. She didn't have the strength to open the door.

"Come have a seat, please."

By now the class was cognizant of what was going on. The show had drawn the interest of everybody. There was no longer an interest in hearing me read, but rather to continue snacking and watch the live action that was unfolding before their very eyes.

Autumn stomped over to my desk and picked up the phone. Again with gritted teeth she yelled at me, "I'm gonna call my mom."

"OK, great."

Well, lucky for me she didn't know that you had to dial nine first to get an outside line. So, she punched all kinds of numbers on the phone with no luck. I went about the room trying to put things away and let her cool down. I heard Kip, who by no means was a rule follower himself, say, "Autumn, you shouldn't talk to Mr. McGowan that way. He is the teacher."

"I don't care! I act like this because I know Mr. McGowan did when he was in school."

"No, I didn't, Autumn. I followed the procedures at school and tried to get along with my teachers." (Sometimes telling a lie seems like right thing. This happened to be exactly one of those times. Autumn was right. I had been a complete handful as a child in school. It didn't seem like this was the time to let her in on that.)

"I bet you did when you were in pre-school."

"I didn't go to pre-school."

"You didn't?!?"

"No. My mom wouldn't let me go."

"She wouldn't?!?!"

For the first time in about ten minutes she was stumped. She didn't know what to say. She had no comeback. I was glad because I really didn't know what to say or know what to do with her. As the teacher you can't make anyone do anything. A child has to decide if they are going to go along with what you say, follow directions and the routines you have established, or if they are going to go AWOL.

Autumn sat at my desk and began going through my desk drawers. I think this was largely just for effect. I went about moving the class onto Writers Workshop. Before long Autumn hung her bag back up and sat down at her table on her own. She began to write a story. This was the end of our confrontation.

BZZZ! The alarm sounded. A white light flashed feverishly on the fire indicator in room eleven. All the kids lined up at the door and we headed outside to our designated line up spot. I was absolutely amazed at how no child in the entire school made a sound. Each and every line was single file. I charged ahead of my class leading them to safety from the mock inferno. I was the only teacher in sight. There was a huge red emergency backpack that each teacher carried with a list of all the student's names, parents phone numbers, first aid materials, a flashlight, and a zillion other essential items for any emergency you could dream of. I had the backpack slung over my right shoulder. The kids lined up outside on the playground directly behind a yellow number eleven that had been painted on the blacktop. Each emergency backpack held a red and green double-sided flag. Amy, the first student in our line, placed our green flag up. This signified that all the students in our room were accounted for. A few minutes before the alarm Kevin had managed to talk me into granting permission for him to visit the nurse in the school clinic. He hadn't returned to room eleven prior to the alarm. Hopefully the nurse was wheeling his cot out the front door as we emptied room eleven from the rear of the school. Officer Lakewood came swooping around the lines of students with her usual look of concern. When she got to my class, she marked off on a checklist that the students in room eleven were accounted for. What was to follow blew me away. At my "old school" we would wait until the secretary came on the intercom and said, "Come on in." At my new school on Mercer Island every single child, teacher, support staff, volunteer and visitor who registered at school that day had to be accounted for before we could return to the building. The secretary read from the list of names of people who had signed in as visitors and volunteers over the walkie-talkie that Officer Lakewood had on her wrist. Officer Lakewood yelled out each name to verify that they were here and lined up with the kids. The entire process took about twenty minutes. There wasn't a sound or movement from any student. Mrs. Lakewood's assistant, Dan, came over to my line.

"Joby, where is Kevin?"

"He is in the clinic."

"Your flag shows green. Green means everyone is here."

"Yes, everyone is here. I know where Kevin is. So, I put up our green flag."

Apparently the S.O.P. manual states that if a child is not directly with you, even if you know where they are, put up the red flag so they can be accounted for elsewhere. I flunked my first fire drill.

An e-mail from Officer Lakewood followed the fire drill from reminding staff about the procedures for fire drills. She refreshed our memories that teachers and staff were to be sure to walk at the end of the line to ensure that all students left the building and that nobody remained inside. It seemed unlikely that any child in primary school would want to stay in a burning building, but it did explain why I was the only teacher I saw on the playground as I charged in front of my class as we exited the school building. Everyone else was at the end of his or her line.

It wasn't long before more concerns with homework rolled in. Levon's mother, Mrs. Sneth, contacted me shortly after the homework with time and measurement came sailing home. On Levon's homework was a note scrawled in pencil, "Please contact me at once regarding this. It was a miracle in itself that I even saw the note. I had placed zero emphasis or merit on homework and had fallen into the forbidden practice of dumping the homework in the recycle bin the minute it was returned to school. In the ever so professional way that teachers do, I pulled Levon aside and I asked, "What is this all about?"

"My dad is really mad at you."

"Oh? What about?"

"He is just really mad about the homework. We don't have the stuff we need to do the pages in the packet."

I wondered if, in my haste, I had thrown in something that required materials that were not included. It was highly likely that I had. I dismissed Levon and rummaged through the recycle bin to find his packet. There was a paper ruler photocopied on the side of one of the sheets that the kids were supposed to cut out and use to measure the items on the page. Levon's was not cut out. Armed with this information I called Levon over again.

"Levon, there is a ruler here on the side of the page. You were supposed to cut it out and use it to measure the things on the sheet. It tells you that in the directions."

"Oh. I didn't know that."

In an effort to save myself from going nutty over the "Please contact me at once" note from Mrs. Sneth, I decided that I would e-mail her. This would provide documentation of our communication. She wrote back without any sign of comprehension. I tried to re-explain that all materials were available in the packet. Everything he needed was there. She still didn't compute. On the third e-mail communication of the day between Mrs. Sneth and I it was clear that she was nuts. Upon receiving the fourth inquiry from her that day I simply did not respond. There is something tiring about repeatedly throwing out a lifeline for someone who has been sinking for years. It was obvious that this lack of mental wherewithal had started long before I ever met her. She sunk. I stayed afloat. Hopefully someone else would be able to rescue her dumb ass. I added her name to the list of things I hated.

I determined that it was time to put an end to the homework hullabaloo. I drafted a letter to parents saying that whatever they wanted homework to signify for their child would be fine with me. If they did not want their kids to do any homework, they didn't have to. If they wanted their kids to do the standard thirty minutes each night they should have them read for fifteen then work in the packet for fifteen and stop. If they believed their kids needed more than thirty minutes of homework they should work in the packet for a longer stretch of time. I would completely support whatever they wanted homework to signify for their kids. If the homework I sent home was not enough they might want to consider buying a workbook at an educational store in the area. There were no more questions about homework for the rest of the year. I finally won. I was in the mood to take names and kick some Poverty Rock ass.

Feeling the pressure from parents who were dying to get in and volunteer I sent an e-mail inviting any parent who wanted to come and read to the class to let me know. We could arrange a time to do so. A few parents took me up on it. Jim's mom came and read entertaining stories with enthusiasm and great reading rhythm. Darrin's grandfather visited room eleven to read. Natalie's grandmother and grandfather both made arrangements to read. It was very exciting and noteworthy for students to have family members in to read. It also helped send the message that reading wasn't just a skill to be successful at in school. It provided an opportunity for the students to learn more about reading in the area of fluency, enunciation, rhythm, expressiveness, etc. Ken's mom and dad had both come to read. Ken's dad e-mailed and said he wanted to set up a weekly time to come and read to the kids. Uh oh. The pressure was on for me to cook up a weekly schedule for volunteers. I agreed. He was scheduled to come each Wednesday morning at 9:30 and read for ten to fifteen minutes. I selected picture books on a variety of topics for him to read. One of the early books I selected was *Smoky Night*. It described the Los Angeles riots from the early 90's. A few pages into the book Ken's dad questioned the appropriateness of the book. I urged him to continue reading. When he finished it proved to be a great springboard for dialog and conversation in room eleven. The kids had many ideas and things to talk about. Someone brought up the Seattle riots from a few years earlier. I used to believe that sheltering kids was the best way to handle difficult subjects. I am learning that sometimes putting it out in the open to talk about it proves to be the best way to find out how kids feel about situations and how they process different emotions.

Ken's dad came to read several more times. On one visit he handed the book back to me and said, "This is too short. I need a longer book." I looked at him. I looked at the clock and said, "You are ten minutes late. This is all we have time for." Obviously he didn't realize the importance of our time because he had stopped for a Starbucks coffee on the way. He was holding a Grande latte in his right hand. I suspected this was what held him up. A pattern emerged. He was late many times. The next week when he arrived he looked put out with the book selection I had made. Sensing his disgust for my ability to select appropriate literature I said, "Why don't you come early, stop at the library and pick out a book that you want to read to the class. We have ten to fifteen minutes for your reading on Wednesdays. Maybe you should pick out a chapter book and read one chapter or two each week when you come." By cracky, he thought that was a splendid idea. I think he figured out I was tired of his free advice.

By the end of September I had a lingering feeling of regret. Regret for leaving Iowa. Regret for not being stronger. Regret for not letting things roll off my back. Being on the defense is not such a great way to live or work.

It was time for our first field trip. We were scheduled to walk to the Mercer Island Water Tower and the Mercer Island Public Library. Somewhere in the back of my mind I knew arranging chaperones would be a nightmare in itself. I sent out an e-mail to the families of room eleven asking for the first five volunteers who would be willing to go along. By the end of the day I had responses from fifteen parents desiring to go. I selected the first five and informed the others that they would be welcome to come on at least one trip before the end of the year, but thanks for the interest.

As I built the list for which students would go with which parent I took special care to ensure that Mrs. Craston had the four highest maintenance students in room eleven. Why not? She was confident that she knew how the classroom should be run. I wanted to give her an opportunity to shine as a teacher. There was a huge sense of satisfaction watching her lead the class with her small posse of students up the hill of the school parking lot and down the street.

As we arrived at the Mercer Island Water Tower one of the kids proclaimed they were thirsty. The fellow who gave the less than stellar tour of the facility took the kids outside. Using a wrench he opened up the valve on a fire hydrant. Shortly after, a huge gush of water came spewing out of the hydrant. I think I must have had a look of utter despair as I watched five of the second graders race through the force of water, pushing them forward. Others tried to put their mouth in the stream. I was astonished as all the parent volunteers stood around exhibiting zero effort to help regain control of the situation. It did not seem to be a big deal that kids were soaking themselves in the water and that in all actuality there was the possibility of someone becoming injured by the hurricane force of water roaring out of the hydrant. After the shock wore off I clapped my loud hands together and demanded that everyone step away from the hydrant. This went down in the book of field trip hell.

We headed down the street, some of us dripping, to the public library. A tour, story, and scavenger hunt were on the agenda. The kids enjoyed themselves thoroughly. About half way through the field trip Mrs. Craston started pestering me about the time and how long it would take us to walk back to school. She proclaimed that we were cutting it too close. She kept remarking about the time to anyone who would listen. Nobody listened to her constant dribble. That part felt good. Finally I told her that we would be fine and to please stop worrying. If the kids sensed her frustration it would send an uncomfortable message to them. I wanted the kids to enjoy the experience fully without having to endure her psychotic behavior.

As we left the library she charged ahead of the pack with her four students from room eleven insisting that we needed to hurry back or the students would miss the dismissal busses. What a spaz. A bee on the way back stung only one student. There were five wet kids and only one bee sting. All in all it was a great trip.

Jacob was a popular student in our class. He stood taller than most kids in second grade. He was a sports guru. He could play basketball, soccer, football, and always managed to have terrific team spirit and maintained a positive attitude. His mother, Nancy, wrote…

"Joby, Jacob loves your class. He informs people he has the "cool, new, tall teacher who is really great!" I was so impressed with the incredible control you have over the class already. I thought they were out of the room when I first arrived yesterday because they were so quiet. Amazing! I would love to come in and read again some time when it works for you."

Jacob and his mom were added to the list of things I enjoyed. It was a short list.

# OCTOBER 2002

I received an e-mail from Ken's mom, Larissa, early in October. It read,

"I wanted to write and let you know that your efforts working with Ken have really paid off. I think he is really growing up. He is beginning to take personal responsibility for himself on some things like getting ready for soccer, being respectful, and working on being the best person he can be."

Well, great for Ken. I couldn't figure out why I was receiving this e-mail. Then half way through the e-mail the kicker came. The first part of the e-mail was fluff. The meat of the matter was here.

"Also, I wanted to know if you have thought about putting together a group or an opportunity for some more challenging reading and spelling for some of the kids. I know Ken would appreciate the challenge. Thanks for everything you do."

No. I haven't thought about putting together a more "challenging" list of spelling words. Have you thought about shutting the hell up?

My father was diagnosed with brain cancer in June of that year. I received word one afternoon early in October that he had taken a turn for the worse. He was now in a wheel chair and bed ridden to the main floor of his home. I felt it would be wise to take a trip home and visit for a few days, as the end seemed to be in sight. I skated up to Officer Lakewood's office to ask permission to miss a few days of school. With great concern and support she insisted that I take time and go home to visit my father. I began to re-evaluate my distaste for her. It was possible that she had a sensitive side. I made airline reservations and prepared materials for three days of school. I told the kids I would be out for a few days and that they would be having a guest teacher. Mrs. Best, who had taught second grade at the school for a zillion years recently retired and had agreed to cover the class. I flew out the following morning. The one good thing about being away from school was that I missed the second fire drill of the year. Not to worry, though. There were eight more to come.

Upon my return from Iowa the voicemail light on my phone was blinking. As you might have guessed Craston was gravely concerned with the guest teacher, Mrs. Best. Apparently she yelled as much as I did in the eyes of Mrs. Craston. I decided to award Mrs. Best two thumbs up. Thank you Mrs. Best for being a hard ass like me.

I had been back to school a few days from visiting my dad when I was working with a few students at the football table. Each table in the room was designated as a different sport team. Some kids sat at the soccer team table, others were at the baseball, football, and referee tables. Lucy and Maya were two students who I enjoyed thoroughly. They were working on a project together at the table next to me. Maya had spunk. She had remarkable creativity. Her empathy for peers and adults was like none other. She was full of great ideas and always eager to have a great time. She enjoyed visiting with her pack of friends and with me.

Lucy was an incredible girl who read and computed math problems well beyond many children her age. Lucy longed for more knowledge and experience. She was always eager to ask why and how. Lucy showed signs that she liked me. It was nice to know that at least one of the kids liked me, even though Craston was convinced that I was the worst teacher. I happened to overhear their conversation that day. Maya was explaining about one of her relatives who just had a baby. The conversation went like this…

"My aunt had a baby. They had to cut her stomach open to get it out."

Lucy had a look of bewilderment on her face as she tipped her head to the side almost unable to believe what she had just heard. After a minute she said, "That's nothing! My dad, he just shot

32

right out of my grandma's butt!"

Maya: "They do! They just shoot right out!"

Lucy: "I don't know how my aunt got out of my grandma's stomach, though."

I remember thinking, after bringing my oxygen level back up, that these were the reasons why I taught. Enjoying kid's stories and their perspectives on life were the things that made this job the greatest experience of my life. Hopefully I would remember that in the future when the next atomic bomb went off with another parent or Officer Lakewood.

Mrs. Craston and I had shared enough entanglements to last me a lifetime. I had met Mr. Craston at Curriculum Night. I had never seen or heard from him since that time until I received the following e-mail.

"Thanks for the newsletters. E-mail is such a great tool for communicating with parents and I'm so glad you use it. Mike has been very excited about school lately and is really enjoying you as a teacher. Thanks and keep up the good work. Mike and I will be sure to watch for the moon on our camping trip this weekend. (We had begun a unit on the Phases of the Moon just a week before.) Thanks again."

Well, obviously Mr. Craston knew that his wife was nuts. This was a mop up e-mail. Whatever the reason, I appreciated that Mr. Craston was not as crazy as his wife.

# LATE OCTOBER 2002

I was beginning to think that we could all use some lighter air around the prison. So, I sashayed up to the office one Friday afternoon a few minutes after 4:00. I had grown to appreciate the school's new secretary, Lee. She too was living her first year at the school. We had shared brief moments in hell together and had somehow figured out that each other was in pain working at the school. I asked for permission to use the intercom. She smiled, dialed the secret intercom code and handed me the phone.

"May I have your attention please? This will serve as the final boarding call for United Airlines flight 271 with non-stop Boeing 757 jet service to Denver. All confirmed and standby passengers should now be on board the aircraft for an immediate departure through Gate C12. Once again, Final call United flight 271 service to Denver, gate C12, All aboard."

Before I got to the part of the speech where I announced which gate all passengers should board through, Officer Lakewood, clipboard in hand, walkie-talkie tied to her wrist and key chain slung around her other wrist, flew into the office with the look of frustration on her face. This was her usual look, loaded up with the clipboard, walkie-talkie and keys. The frown was typical as well. I knew this time that the frown was all for me. (Though I never figured out the exact contents of the papers on the clipboard, my best guess is that it contained a list of staff members and a place to tally the number of infractions each staff member made during the course of the year. The walkie-talkie was so that she could be in constant contact with the front office.)

"Joby, I am concerned about which parents might be in the building that I would have to explain this to." Translation: Having a sense of humor, let alone a personality of your own, is not appreciated here.

Officer Lakewood didn't care for the show of personality in my speech. Somewhere in the neighborhood of ten staff members cheered and headed for the front office as if it were Gate C12. I was starting to like the brave souls who showed face, ready to board, while I got a speech about appropriate use of the intercom from Officer Lakewood. E-mails of appreciation followed from fellow teachers and staff expressing their delight with my light sense of humor. I guess when you are in prison anything seems fun to your fellow inmates.

We were ready to have a school wide assembly. Kindergarten and first grade students sat on the floor on mats up front. Second through fifth grade students brought their chairs to assemblies. This was a new idea for me. I was accustomed to having all kids sit on the floor with no mats. As you might have guessed the entire procedure was outlined in the S.O.P. manual. There were specific directions about which hallway each class was supposed to use when coming to an assembly and which door to the gymnasium you were to enter. Room one entered first, then room two, three, and so on. You were not to enter the gymnasium until every room before you had already been seated. What it boiled down to was a huge back up in the hallways. As you entered the gymnasium Officer Lakewood checked off your class from another one of her lists. She directed you where to sit.

At the end of the first assembly the student body from room eleven was ready to head out. We had just exited the gymnasium and I remembered thinking, "Where is Lakewood?" We swung around the corner and there she was. Her hand was up giving room eleven the signal to halt. She stopped my class because we were not carrying our chairs in the prescribed manner as laid out in the S.O.P. manual. I kept thinking when things like this happened that I really needed to make reading the S.O.P. manual a top priority. Apparently it was not safe to carry the chairs with the seat back to your stomach. They should be carried sideways, so the back of the chair was to the child's side. Mental note to self: Don't screw that up next time. As my class got the speech for how to properly carry their chairs in the "safest" manner, other classes were sailing by us holding their chairs in the prescribed manner.

Immediately before school started one morning in October Amy walked in the classroom with a woman wearing a tent like dress. The woman, holding Amy by her wrist, walked up to me and said,

"I am Amy's nanny. We are here to help teach Amy how to be responsible about bringing her homework home. I am going to show her how to pack her school bag."

One thing I was for sure on was that Amy knew how to pack her bag. She had been doing it for nearly two and a half years now. I figured if Nanny needed to prance in the room and make a display of how good she was at "teaching", then so be it. Through nanny's actions she must have been trying to communicate how poor of a job she thought I had done teaching kids to be responsible because Amy didn't have her homework and other things when she came home. I need to clear the air on one thing. It is not the teacher's responsibility to make sure each child packs their bag each night after school. It could be construed as an invasion of privacy if I go digging through student bags to make sure they have everything they need. Aside from that, if you don't have what you need, then be ready to face the consequence. Why are we rescuing so many kids from responsibility? I let nanny do her thing and I excused myself to head up to the office.

Halloween was a big deal on Mercer Island. All the kids dressed up. I did too. They all were excited to see what McGowan had cooked up for a costume. I went to Target and bought some silk bullet pajamas. They were the most comfortable things I have ever owned. I sloshed around in those and my stocking feet for the party. There were games and snacks and all kinds of things for the kids to do. There was loose organization of the party, yet I was amazed at how the kids all were entertained and engaged. Apparently kids were free to roam from station to station. The kids knew this without any direction from the room parents.

Craston was in full swing that afternoon. She was directing the piñata breaking and the snack table. She was a blur running from station to station undermining every other adult that was there. I plopped my big self down at a table and did cross words with Jacob and Lucy.

# NOVEMBER 2002

My dad passed away on November 8, 2002. I phoned Officer Lakewood at home that evening to explain that I would be away to attend services and assist my family for at least one week. Again, she expressed sincere concern for my family and asked what she could do to help. I boarded a flight headed to Iowa. There was an outpouring of support and help from the staff during my time away and again upon my return. Nearly every family represented in room eleven sent cards, e-mails and words of care and kindness.

Immediately upon returning from my dad's funeral and time with family we launched into parent – teacher conferences. The greatest gift was that the five school days prior to Thanksgiving were noon release. Kids left at noon. Teachers held conferences with families from noon – 3:30. At my "old school" you hosted the conferences on your own time after school dismissed in the afternoon. Every year as a teacher you have at least one sleeper. A sleeper is a parent who has not yet come to you about their concerns, rather just held onto them so they can blast you when they visit you in person at the conference itself. This year was no different. After listening to countless parents talk about homework and the usual dribble about their being too much, not enough, no challenges, the work being too difficult, and my not being like the other second grade teachers did I managed to squeeze in some dialog about student behavior, academic progress and other issues.

Midway through the conference week Autumn had her conference. Autumn was one who I had grown to be proud of in many ways. We had come to a working agreement. She did follow through on procedures and routines. There were no more conflicts between us and we had somehow managed to respect one another. I was appreciating her sense of humor. Her thinking and processing skills were far beyond what I would have expected from a second grader. Autumn came with her mom and dad to the conference. She sat on the floor and played with blocks while mom, dad, and I reviewed her academic progress. At the close of the conference I asked Autumn to clean up her blocks.

"You pick those up you little boy!" she yelled, as she pointed her finger, at her dad. I stood in amazement as her dad bent over and cleaned up her mess while Autumn and mom walked hand in hand out the door of room eleven.

# DECEMBER 2002

Lori, a fourth grade teacher, told me one day, "You know it is going to be a good day when your red voicemail light isn't blinking on your phone." These were words of gospel truth.

I arrived at school one morning in early December. The red light on the phone was blinking. Some days I shuffled papers around and put them so the corners would cover the upper right corner of the phone so I couldn't see the red light. The ringer was always turned off. I dialed in to get the voicemail messages. There was a message from Samantha's mom. Was I aware of the incident yesterday at lunch where another girl in room eleven told Samantha she couldn't sit with her at lunch? Well, damn. I wasn't aware of the situation. Nor did I think this was something that merited much attention. I deleted the e-mail and debated how I would respond, if at all. Contacting someone on the phone was risky. If they were home and answered you might never get off of the phone. If you e-mailed them there was written documentation, which could prove to be beneficial or come back to kick you in the ass later. So, I swallowed my hope and phoned her back. We had a charming chat. I assured Samantha's mother that indeed I would look into it and visit with the girls who were involved. I also urged her to tell Samantha to come talk to me anytime she felt threatened by a peer. After all it is my job to help kids learn how to talk through what they are feeling and experiencing with peers. What better way to help these kids learn strategies to cope with stress than to take real life, every day situations and guide them through the problem solving process. I too learned from the situation about what my role should be and to maybe lighten up when someone called with a situation that seemed trivial.

"Mr. McGowan! The drinking fountain is broken!" Kip informed me in a level four voice. Yes, there were voice levels as dictated by Officer Lakewood. Voice level zero meant no voices. Level one was a whisper and so on. I wished that things would break at more convenient times. During the middle of a Guided Reading Group wasn't the best, for me. I stopped the group and walked over to the fountain to take a look. Someone had shoved a chocolate chip down the hole where the water fountains out. Instantly I knew we had a drinking fountain crisis in room eleven. The attention of all twenty-three students was now off of the language arts task at hand and focused directly on me. Some were curious to see how I would handle this latest development. Others were thrilled that there was something else to focus on aside from their work. A small crowd had gathered back at the drinking fountain.

As a teacher I ask some of the most profound questions at

times. Case in point, once I discovered the chocolate chip in the fountain I asked in my best teacher voice, "People, who plugged up the fountain with a chocolate chip?" If criminals confessed this easily there wouldn't be a need for a justice system. Nobody confessed. I took the palm of my hand and hit the fountain button with force to try and dislodge the chocolate chip. Success! The chip flew out of the fountain and nailed me on the side of my head, along with a large gush of water. Instant irritation flooded me as the entire class burst out laughing.

"I will need to know who is responsible for this chocolate chip deal by the end of the day. There will be a consequence."

It was now silent. Time for lunch.

While the kids were at lunch, Adam, our PE teacher, stopped by to shoot the breeze for a few minutes. I told him the story of the chocolate chip. Adam had some of the most interesting ideas I had ever heard of. The kids are often entertained by his antics, stories and general state of upbeat positive energy. This is what he said, "McGowan, this is what we are going to do. We will put a marker up in the ceiling tile and point the tip out just a half of an inch. When the kids come in from lunch recess I will be here and tell them that whoever did the chocolate chip thing needs to confess by the end of today because we have it all on video tape (the marker was supposed to be the camera). It would be a shame if Mr. McGowan had to watch the tape to find out who it was, but he will if nobody confesses."

Adam had some crazy ideas. This topped the list. I was not convinced that we could actually get the kids to believe that the lid of this black marker was the lens of a video camera. I thought, what the hell? If he were going to be in charge of it and tell the kids, I would go along with it.

The kids filed in from the noon recess a few minutes later. Adam gathered the kids over by the fountain and explained the entire situation to them. They all stared up at the ceiling to see the "camera". Hook, line, and sinker they bought every word of it. Adam was smooth. Mental note to self: Don't discredit PE teachers as complete slackers so much.

The kids were in a panic.

"Mr. McGowan, when will you watch the videotape?

"At the end of the school day."

"What will happen to whoever did it?"

"There will be a consequence."

"What will the consequence be?"

" I haven't decided. It will be private between the student who is responsible and myself."

There was silence in room eleven. I liked that part. The wheels of twenty-three second graders were turning at full speed. I imagined that most were trying to figure out who was responsible for the chocolate chip fountain trick. I am sure the rest of the kids were trying to determine what Judge McGowan would render as a reasonable consequence when the tight-lipped chocolate chip culprit was caught. We were back to work. Every few minutes someone would come up, tap me, and ask in a whisper, "Did anyone tell you who did it yet?" About an hour later as the class worked on a math computation story problem, Kip stood at my desk. The conversation went like this…

"What if you know who jammed the chocolate chip in the drinking fountain?"

"Well, Kip, I hope the person who did it will tell me themselves."

"If you know who did it, should you tell?"

"You will have to decide that for yourself. If you think you need to tell me, then do. If you don't, then I trust that the person who is responsible will tell me."

"Are you going to call their parents?"

"I don't know."

"What will the consequence be?"

"I don't know. Kip, do you know who is responsible?"

"Yes."

"Kip, was it you?"

"Yes."

A huge sense of relief came over me. It wasn't because I had cracked the case of the chocolate chip fountain. It was the fact that if nobody coughed up responsibility by the end of the day I had let Adam, PE teacher of the year, talk me into this insane story about the camera and videotape. It was a highly unlikely scenario that room eleven was equipped like a 7-11. I also had scenes flash through my mind that afternoon of twenty-three kids at dinner tables all across Mercer Island explaining how Mr. McGowan was probably at home right this very minute watching the tape of who jammed the chocolate chip in the drinking fountain because nobody confessed. For sure the red light would be blinking on the phone the following morning regardless of the day's outcome.

I thanked Kip for telling me and explained that I would need some time to think about how I would handle this. I would let him know what the consequence would be after the last recess that day. I think the sheer fact that he had to wait an hour and a half to find out what I would determine as a fair and reasonable punishment was punishment enough in itself. I told Kip how appreciative I was that he told me the truth and that since this was his first offense we would let it go provided there were no more incidents in the future. He thanked me and agreed. He was smiling again. So was I. The red voicemail light did not blink the next morning.

Staff meetings were a real treat. Without fail they were held every Thursday morning at 8:00 sharp. Officer Lakewood stood at the front of the room and checked off those who attended and wrote down the names of those who did not as well as those who arrived late. If you were late, or did not attend a staff meeting you were the recipient of a surprise visit accompanied by an in depth interrogation as to your whereabouts at the time of the meeting from Officer Lakewood later that day.

This particular staff meeting was dedicated to many things. One of the top priorities was centered on procedures. God only knows why. There were at least eight zillion of them in the S.O.P. manual, which I still hadn't read. The most pressing procedure to discuss was the use of the library by students during lunch recesses. If students opted not to go to the playground during lunch recess, they could come to the library and read quietly, check out books, etc. Officer Lakewood was instituting a new policy for which library door the kids should exit if they were leaving the library during recess, but before the recess bell rang. If students left the library to go back outside for recess before recess time had ended and it was before 12:55 they should use the North exit from the library and use the northeast exit to the school itself to get to the playground. If they left the library after 12:56 and were going outside to recess, they should use the south exit of the library and the southeast exit of the building to get to the playground. There were similar rules discussed for each of the three recess shifts. I struggled to understand the reasoning, nor did I even really want to. So, instead I offered my opinion,

"There are too many procedures here." I got dagger eyes and what I am sure was my name written down as Officer Lakewood began writing something on the infamous clipboard. Didn't anyone else think these recess door rules were over the edge?

It was a wet, rainy winter afternoon in December when Mike got bonked in the head with a metal lunch box while lined up waiting to come inside from recess. Of all the kids to get zonked on the head, why did it have to be him? I ushered him to the nurse's office for ice and documentation of the incident. I screwed up my courage and e-mailed Mrs. Craston so she would know what happened. I was ready for a backlash from her. It never came. Thank you God.

Shortly before the Winter 2002 Break we were all issued badges by the school district with our picture printed smack dab in the center and our assigned school building indicated on the badge. I managed to get a hold of Adam's, our PE teacher, and photocopied his picture. I used the Xerox machine to blow it up to 5"x6" in size. Then I craftily whipped up a poster titled "WANTED". I slapped his mug on it and ran about 10 copies. I posted them all over the staff lounge and in the staff restrooms. The Gestapo, headed by Officer Lakewood, removed every poster within ten minutes of their being posted. I am sure another check mark was added to my name on the clipboard.

# JANUARY 2003

It was time for a program called Terrific Books to begin. Mrs. Craston had contacted me numerous times since the beginning of the year demanding to know when I would have this program up and running in room eleven. Parent volunteers ran Terrific Books. Each week students would read one book and meet to discuss various aspects of the specific book. Parents would lead small groups of four to six children each. As you might have guessed Mrs. Craston was expecting to be one of the parents. I had no trouble obtaining volunteers for the program.

I spent a significant amount of time putting together groups of students that were balanced between boys and girls. The groups had representation of different ethnicities. Each group had students who were strong as well as students who struggled as readers. In creating the groups it didn't work out to have each of the parent volunteers work with their child's group. Mrs. Craston self appointed herself as leader of the program for room eleven. Thanks. Mrs. Craston e-mailed me the following,

"Hi Joby. I'm not sure how happy parents will be with this. That's why parents sign up with the program (so they can do it with their kids) and that's why most kids want to do Terrific Books. To keep parents and kids happy I really would recommend trying to keep parents with their own kids. I think it would generate a more positive outcome and feelings that the other way around since parents are going into this and signed up for this thinking they would be with their own child. (Remember, parents have been telling their kids this as a selling point to the program!) Maybe training for Terrific Books should be part of the "New Teacher Orientation!""

As the bullshit deepened she went on to explain how I should have organized the groups. Furthermore, I had gotten too many volunteers. It wouldn't work to have seven parents working with groups. The groups would be too small. I should tell Kevin's mom that she wouldn't be able to volunteer for Terrific Books this year. Well, no matter whom she suggested that I tell they couldn't volunteer I would have bucked her because Craston and I already had such a great working relationship. The fact of the matter was that I adored Kevin. He brought spunk and sunshine to our room. He was such a great kid with enthusiasm and energy to help light our class on fire. The last person I was going to dismiss from the group would be his mother. So, in my less than collected manner I wrote her back the following,

"This is beginning to take a large amount of my time. It is frustrating to continually try and meet the expectations of so many different groups. There are so many different wants and desires from parents, the school, fellow staff, the kids, etc. It is difficult to juggle what everyone wants all of the time. For example, take the homework. There are so many different expectations from parents. Some want more. Some want none. Some think there should be more math assignments. Others say there is too much math homework. Some want me to make special separate homework for their child for multiple reasons. The bottom line is that there is only one of me and I can only do so much. Everyone who approaches me says that what they want is "what the parents want". It is getting difficult to juggle all of the "wants". I put a significant amount of time and thought into making the groups for Terrific Books. There are a wide range of behaviors in our class, ability levels, and interests represented by the kids. What people often forget is that all of these other factors come into play aside from just what they "want" to see happen. How about you put the kids together into groups. Whatever you feel is fine will work for me. I need to be spending time on other things that are pertinent to what I am supposed to be teaching and doing."

Clicking send was a cleansing act. I needed time to breathe and not think about Mrs. Craston. I went to lunch. When I returned there was another e-mail from her.

Her brief response read, "I am sorry to have upset you so much. I will work things out and let you know when the groups are put together." Terrific Books began a week or so later and I didn't speak to her on her visits. I had learned a new strategy for dealing with P.I.T.A. parents. (Pain in the Ass) Ignoring them and not speaking to them was completely freeing. I talked to everyone else who showed up and was resolved that the best way to deal with her was to not. Terrific Books continued for six long weeks.

Half way through the Terrific Books program I received an e-mail from Noor's dad. The Terrific Books were too easy. It didn't seem appropriate that the kids were reading a book about a Disney story. Would I please select more difficult materials? I replied and explained that the books were not selected based on reading ability. Rather, the books were selected to provide opportunities for discussion within the small groups. The books were supposed to be easy. I explained that it was a parent volunteer program. Parents handled every decision about the program. In a return e-mail from Noor's dad he expressed concern that a parent would make educational decisions for the students in the classroom that I was the teacher of. I urged him to contact Mrs. Craston, self-appointed Terrific Books Leader of room eleven. I forwarded the copy of his e-mail to cat hair woman. Why not? She should deal with the frustration of parents for the mess she had created. I was tired. I didn't give two flips about Terrific Books. Noor's dad quickly figured out that Mrs. Craston had squashed me on more than one occasion and was muscling me around to get her way. I was giving in to shut her up. I had just earned the trust and confidence of Noor's parents. They were completely supportive of me and were all too familiar with the somewhat unrealistic expectations that could crop up on Mercer Island from some parents. I began to realize that some parents were not crazy and that I indeed did have supporters.

I was glad to see Terrific Books come to an end.

One evening after school had released late in January, Mrs. Sneth bobbed into room eleven. She had Levon's grandmother with her.

Mrs. Sneth: "How's Levon doing?" Don't parents know that when you ask a blanket question like "How's he doing?" that it really doesn't ask you anything?

She introduced me to Levon's grandmother. She had some information for me as well.

"Yes, I am a teacher and have been for many years. I am concerned about Levon's math computation. I am here so you will show Levon's mom the tests you use to asses the students. I use assessments when teaching my students. She needs to see these."

I explained that some assessments were used across curricular areas. The school and curriculum did not provide assessments for every aspect of the curriculum. I went on to note that math computation (math facts and timed tests) were not part of the mandated second grade curriculum. I explained that all student work comes home with Levon on a daily basis.

I asked, "Where do you teach and what grade?"

"Oh, I am a substitute teacher now. I am retired. I teach all grades."

Well, so much for her theory of currently using assessments of the students she teaches. I went on to explain that Levon's behavior was less than satisfactory. Levon had hooked up with two buddies in our class. The three of them struggled to adhere to procedures and routines in the classroom. Without fail on a consistent basis one of the three would be up at one of the other person's table, visiting, scheming, etc. I explained that there was significant room for growth with this behavior.

Mom and Grandma were shocked. They had no indication that Levon had struggled with these types of behavior in prior classes. Mental note to self: Check cum file to see what Levon's behavior was like in the past. In reviewing his file I found comments on nearly every reporting period in Kindergarten and first grade about his behavior, lack of time spent on task, etc. It looked as though ma and granny had Alzheimer's.

Ken's dad continued to read each Wednesday morning from 9:30 to 9:45. One Wednesday in January he approached me and explained that he would like to bring in twenty-three hot chocolates prepared at Starbucks the next week he came to read. I stood there in silence. I am sure the look on my face told it all.

48

I quickly regained my perma-grin and said, "Sure, you bet. If you can figure out a way to get Starbucks to make twenty-three hot chocolates and get them here to school on time for the 9:30 read aloud you go for it." OK, he thought he would. I think reality must have hit sometime during the week after he left because we never did have those twenty-three cups of hot chocolate. Fine by me.

Near the end of January it was time to prepare report forms again. They were sent home. Mrs. Sneth e-mailed me with grave concerns about Levon's report card and wished to schedule a conference. Super! We were going to re-live our live face-to-face meeting we had two weeks earlier.

She arrived with Levon one evening after school a few days later. I figured since she wanted to call the conference I would let her lead it.

"What is it you wanted to talk about?"

"This report card. This is news to me. This behavior. Why haven't you told me about his behavior? He has never had trouble with behavior in the past."

Well, Praise the Lord for cum files. I whipped his out and showed her both the Kindergarten and first grade report cards. I went on to say,

"You and your mother were here two weeks ago and we talked at length about Levon's behavior. It shocks me that you are surprised by the report card."

In the end she asked for a daily note describing the behaviors Levon exhibited, etc. No thanks is what I thought. What I will do is have a notebook for Levon. At the end of each day he will be responsible for writing a few sentences to highlight how things went for him each day. I could read it and then he could take it back and forth between school and home each day. She preferred that I write the letter each day. I explained that I wasn't willing to do so. In an effort to help instill a sense of responsibility and ownership of the problem, Levon would be the one responsible for this, not me. When the hell would I sit down and write about his behavior each day? I was tired of the helicopter parents. This is a parent who files in quickly. It is often after the fact of the matter to tell the teacher what they will do to help their child with a problem or situation that typically is a result of the child's own doing.

The journal worked fine for a few days. Several days passed and I never saw the journal. I received an e-mail from Mrs. Sneth asking why I hadn't sent the journal home in so long. My reply was, "Levon hasn't turned it in to me in several days. It is his responsibility to do so. If you want the journal to continue talk to him about his end of the deal."

The journal began to come in again. All seemed well. It felt as though we were really helping him with responsibility and I was reiterating the message that I was not in charge of his behavior.

Things in the area of behavior began to spiral downward again. There was more time off task, cruising the room, getting drinks, going to the bathroom, lying, etc. One day an incident cropped up involving Levon and one of his buddies. He wrote about it in the journal and sent it home. Too much time was spent visiting with each other in the computer lab. They were unable to complete a four-line poem they were supposed to type. I gauged that they wasted too much time because they were the only two unable to finish the assignment. In all actuality they only had their names on the paper. Levon's buddy, Kip, had the date typed.

I received a phone call from Kip's mother. She explained that she had been called by Levon's mother and was very concerned because clearly Kip had forced Levon to talk. She went on to explain that because of Kip, Levon didn't get his work done. This was a classic case of passing the buck or better known as "helicopter parenting". Now, I had grown to appreciate Kip's mother. She had been supportive since the first day of school with Kip's lack of ability or desire to be on task. She appreciated my high standards for behavior and was supportive to the end. She was frustrated with Mrs. Sneth and wanted me to be aware of what had transpired. I apologized for not having contacted her sooner about the assignment not being completed in the Computer Lab and said I would take it from there.

I e-mailed Mrs. Sneth and said it is with regret that we would no longer be using the communication notebook for Levon. The original intent was to convey Levon's behavior and experience at school each day. I was concerned that she was using it as a forum to point the finger at peers and pass the buck of responsibility. She would have to rely on Levon communicating via word of mouth each day as to how things went. If a serious infraction occurred, I would call her.

I found a note on the floor. It read, "I am going to kill you." For half of a second I thought about throwing it away and ignoring it. Then I thought of Columbine High School and other similar incidents. I asked for the attention of the student body in room eleven. I read the note to them and urged the person who wrote it to see me before the end of the day. I explained how it could be construed as harassment. Of course they all wanted to know, "What will happen to the person who wrote it?" I remember thinking, "I don't know." You can't really admit that kind of thing to the kids. So, I reiterated that there would be a private consequence between the child who wrote it, their parents and myself. Nobody confessed to writing the note by the end of the day.

The next day when I arrived at school my e-mail box was jammed with notes. One in particular was from Ken's dad. He wrote,

"Ken told me about the note. I want to know who the writer was and what was done about it."

Great. I had no idea who wrote it. I tried to do some sleuth work and compare the handwriting on the note to the handwriting in the students' journals. It was nearly impossible to determine who wrote it. We didn't even know whom it was written to. I wrote back to Ken's dad,

"Thanks for your e-mail. As of yet I do not know who the writer is. Once I find out, if I find out, I will inform that child's parent(s) and a consequence will be issued which matches the infraction. Until which time I know who it is, there isn't much I can do. I discussed with the class the severity of the incident. I explained that it is considered to be harassment and that it is highly disturbing. I won't be able to share with you who the writer is unless it turns out to be Ken."

Everybody wants to know who did what! Nobody wants to stand up and yell, "It was me!" Sometimes I wanted to shoot myself for opening up a can of worms like that. We never did find out who the author of the death note was.

The school year was proving to be the most challenging one I had ever had. I had worked with some crazy parents in the past, but nothing like this. I was used to having a building administrator who supported me and had confidence in my classroom management and teaching style. I was pretty sure I didn't have that kind of support here with Officer Lakewood. I began to look for another teaching position. I searched every school district website within twenty miles of Seattle for upcoming teaching vacancies. I dropped the principal of my old school in Iowa an e-mail letting her know that I had an interest in returning if it could all work out. Then I got gutsy. I e-mailed Officer Lakewood and explained that I updated my professional portfolio each school year. Would she be willing to write me a letter of recommendation?

Her e-mail back said, "Sure. Are you looking for another job?"
"Nope. I just want to keep my portfolio updated."

It was revealing, in a sense, what happened about an hour after that. The staff received an e-mail bulletin from Officer Lakewood saying that as we approach the end of the year people will begin to think about other employment options for the next year. Please keep her informed of any changes we were planning to make in an effort to make sure transitions would be smooth at our school. The sooner she knows of our plans, the better she can plan for the following year. Interesting. I had started something. So, I e-mailed her back and said I would like to move to first grade or Kindergarten the next year if possible. My endorsements were in Early Childhood as well as Reading and Language Arts. I missed the early literacy piece by being in second grade. I had no intentions of staying at the school at that time, but didn't include that tidbit of information with the e-mail. I figured I better give her something to chew on so as to divert her hunch that I was thinking about leaving. She wrote back and said, "That is good information to know. We won't know the class makeup until later in the year." I never did get that letter of recommendation from Lakewood.

# FEBRUARY 2003

We had been working on a social studies unit covering the continent of Australia. The kids were enthralled with didgeridoos, kangaroos and everything else that had to do with "Down Under". The kids learned some Aboriginal dances with the help of a guest dance teacher. Once a week we cleared the center of the room so we had a space to leap and jump during the dances. I remember thinking after the first dance lesson that someone was going to be eyeless by the time the lessons concluded in three weeks. Levon, Kip and Joshua leapt and jumped. We were supposed to be imitating the moves of tree frogs. These fellows were kickboxing and using Ninja moves. Jekyll and Hyde had become a regular part of my persona. One minute I was calm and enjoying the kids. The next minute I was irritated with the way a handful of them had no regard for the rules and procedures. Venom often ran from the side of my mouth as I gave looks of death to students who were clearly endangering the lives of others. Australia wasn't so much fun.

It was time to lighten things up again. So, I whipped up a pamphlet one night at home titled "At My Old School". It highlighted all the things that happened at some of the teacher's former schools they had worked at before coming to this school. I scanned photos of teachers and inserted them into the document. It was actually a clever piece of work. I ran a few copies and put them in an envelope taped to the white board in the staff lounge. There were cracks in the pamphlet that ripped, light heartedly, on fellow staff members. Officer Lakewood wasn't too impressed. My sense of humor was not a great addition to her regimented, professional environment that she mandated maintaining.

I remember the day well. It was like God had opened up the windows of heaven and poured out eternal life. At the close of the staff meeting that great Thursday morning Officer Lakewood began to cry and told us after much debate she had decided to retire at the end of the school year. Being in the school had been the absolute best part of her life. It was better than her wedding day, better than the days her kids were born, and better than anything else she had ever experienced. Ahh, yah, that's sick. I was elated. A huge sense of relief poured over me. For the first time all year there was a possible sign of hope. Maybe I could actually work here another year if we had a leader who wasn't

Little Ms. Micromanager. Things were looking up.

# MARCH 2003

It was time to prepare the permission slips for a field trip to the Woodland Park Zoo in Seattle. We had studied rain forests, the animals living in these habitats, and what parts of the globe had such forests. I sent out an e-mail requesting volunteer help from parents who had not yet attended a field trip in an effort to be "fair" so that everyone who wanted to go on a trip was given an opportunity. As usual I had an overwhelming response. I completed the mile high stack of paper work for the trip just as an e-mail came in from Samantha's mom. She didn't make the cut for the trip. I already had enough chaperones. The Woodland Park Zoo in Seattle requested that you bring no more than four adult chaperones. The field trip was provided free of charge to the school through a grant. We needed to follow the guidelines if we accessed this free trip. The e-mail went like this.

"Mr. McGowan, It isn't fair that I don't get to go on the field trip. I don't understand why you can only have four chaperones. Is it because they chaperones get in free? Well, who can stop me from showing up at the zoo at the same time and paying my own entrance fee and going with the class? I am very frustrated. What can we do about this?" Translation: I am going and you can't stop me.

My first reaction was that I could kick her ass. That's what I could do about it. Knowing that a more socially acceptable and professional response would be called for, I wrote back explaining the zoo had guidelines about the number of chaperones because space was limited in some of the areas we visited, cost factors, etc. All in all I would appreciate her support of the guidelines, even if she didn't agree with them. She was someone who checked e-mail about once a month. She must have gotten the e-mail at some point because I never heard another word about it. Thank you God! What the hell is up with field trips? The trips are for the kids. They are not for the parents. I have never worked with a group of people who believed their kid's school years were for them more than for their kids.

# MARCH 11, 2003

I received an e-mail…

"In case anyone hasn't told you lately, you are a terrific teacher. So creative, and so able to keep the kids engaged. Kevin is enjoying your class, and I enjoy what I learn from him. Thanks!"

About the time you think you are ready to run for your life there are gifts. Kevin's parents were my gift that day. I could breathe a sign of relief and know that I had the support of at least one family. No doubt, there were others, but it is much easier to dwell on the two that hate you and forget about the twenty-one sets of parents who do appreciate you. There was ever increasing room for improvement with my attitude.

We were preparing to head home one afternoon. Several kids were hosting a party in the locker area. Others were packing bags and some were still dinking around at their tables. Kip came up to me and said, "Autumn is telling people that you and Maya kissed." Instantly I was pissed. I clapped my big hands together and invited Autumn to come see me in the hall. The conversation went like this…

"Are you telling people that Maya and I kissed?"

She looked pissed at me too, "Yes."

After her confession I walked with Autumn back into room

eleven. I flicked the lights, which has long been a universal signal used by teachers to inform students that it is time to listen up. I launched into my speech with twenty-three sets of eyes staring at me.

"Boys and Girls, Autumn is telling people that Maya and I kissed. Maya, have you and I ever kissed?"

"NO!"

"Boys and Girls, have I ever kissed any of you?"

The whole class in chorus, "No."

"Boys and girls, it makes me very unhappy to have kids saying things that are not true about me. Do you know that I could get in big trouble if kids say this kind of stuff, even if it isn't true?"

Todd, attempting to be Dudley Do-Right, piped up, "You could get fired!"

"Yes, that's right, Todd. I could be fired even if it didn't happen. If one of you goes home and tells your mom and dad that I kiss the kids I could be fired, even if it didn't happen. That makes me angry. I don't ever want to hear this kind of mumbo jumbo again."

My blood pressure was high as I dismissed the kids for home. They were stunned as well I think. The next day, Autumn didn't come to school. There was an e-mail from Autumn's mother awaiting my arrival at school that morning.

"Mr. McGowan, Autumn was very reluctant to go to school today. She wouldn't go. Do you have any idea why she was set on not going?"

As luck would have it, I figured that I knew why. I penned her back and explained the incident from the day before regarding Autumn telling kids that Maya and I were kissing. I was sure that she was afraid to come back today because I was very explicit and firm about how unhappy I was with this lie. Her mother called me within the hour to apologize. She also had Autumn's dad on the phone. This was my first conference call ever. Apparently conference calling is one way in which crisis situations are handled on Mercer Island. Dad wanted to know more about why. I didn't know why, but if we could find out, that would be great. Trying to maintain my excitement for living my very first official conference call, I explained that I had grown to enjoy Autumn's personality. We had some great conversations over the year and that while I was disappointed in what she had said, I still wanted her to come back to school. Autumn returned to school that day by early afternoon.

I received my second conference call later that day. It was Autumn's mom and dad. They wanted to discuss the situation more. Apparently what had happened was that Maya did not want to play with Autumn at recess on the day of the alleged kissing. She told her mom and dad that she made the story up to get back at Maya. I was glad to know what we were dealing with. Mom and dad wanted to talk to Autumn. So, I put Autumn on the phone. There was an instant shut down.

"I want to go home now! You better come and get me now!" I was noticing a pattern in how Autumn talked to her mom and dad. Autumn went into hiding for the remainder of the day by hanging back and avoiding direct contact with me. I decided that in honor of a two conference call day and the resolution of the alleged kissing that I would have a beer when I got home that night.

We started the Giraffe Club Projects at the end of March. The Giraffe Club consisted of people who had stuck their neck out to do something to better the community or the world. We talked about Martin Luther King, Harriet Tubman and many others. The kids were then supposed to create some sort of a Giraffe Club Project to better the community of Mercer Island or some other part of our world. The kids came up with great ideas. Some were planning to clean up trash in local parks every week for four weeks. Some were planning to sell cookies and other things to raise money, which they would donate to homeless shelters. A few students created some gifts to take to a nursing home. Nathan planned to communicate via e-mail with a solider that was overseas fighting the war. Their ideas were impressive. They had a total of six weeks to complete their project. Students were supposed to make a poster or chart or they could write up something to document their work. I e-mailed parents and sent home complete instructions for the project. I looked forward to the creativity that would soon come from the kids.

# APRIL 2003

Well, lucky me. We were preparing to take yet another field trip to the Mercer Island City Hall and Police Station. We had completed a unit earlier in the year on the community of Mercer Island. These trips tied into that unit of study. Mrs. Sneth had attended the zoo field trip the month before. I still had parents who wanted to go on a field trip, but hadn't yet been given the opportunity. I signed up parents who agreed to go. Again I had more volunteers than were needed. Bracing for the potential backlash, I sent an e-mail to the parents stating that I appreciated their support, but I had enough volunteers. There would be a few more trips before the end of the year for those who remained. Mrs. Sneth e-mailed me the following,

"Joby, Please allow me to come on this field trip. It is Levon's birthday and it would mean the world to him. Birthdays are so special and being the only parent I really need to work hard to make sure Levon feels appreciated. Please, please, please allow me to do this. I will not volunteer for any more for fieldtrips unless asked. Please take Levon's special day into consideration.

I look forward to hearing from you." It was signed, Mrs. Sneth.

Ahhh, Yah. First of all, she got re-married a year prior. So, Levon is not in a single parent family. He also saw his biological father frequently and he had a stepfather who lives with him now. Good lie, though. Too bad I am not stupid. As far as never asking to do another thing ever again. I almost believed that but then snapped out of it because nothing with Mrs. Sneth was ever good enough to be true.

I wrote back the following…

"Ms. Sneth, Please do not put me in a position where I am asked to make an exception for you, but not for other parents. Levon's birthday will be special regardless of whether or not you go on the field trip. As I stated in an earlier e-mail to you, if I do not obtain enough parents who have not been on a trip yet, I will open it to those of you who have already gone. I stated in my last e-mail that I would contact you if this becomes the case. It is extremely difficult to try and meet everyone's wants. There are many parents who have not had the opportunity to attend any field trips yet or participate in the parties or Terrific Books Program. You have attended one field trip and been to at least one of the class parties already. I have an obligation to make an effort for those who want to go and have not yet had the opportunity to do so. Thank you for respecting this request and honoring the process I have established for arranging volunteers for this trip. I will let you know if I need your assistance."

Was this woman a nut case, or what? After a short time for reflection I rendered the verdict that indeed she was. That afternoon, Lee, our secretary pulled me aside and asked, "Mrs. Sneth is crazy, isn't she?" Come to find out she had stormed into the school office at 3:30 demanding to see Mrs. Lakewood. She told Lee that she was having a conflict with her son's teacher. Lee said, "Oh, your son has Mr. McGowan. He is a fantastic teacher." Two thumbs up for Lee for sticking up for me. Mrs. Sneth was in Officer Lakewood's office bitching up a storm about me as I walked by the office door. Of course I was preparing my defense for when Officer Lakewood would come down to ask me "How could you make this work for her?" To her credit, she never once mentioned the meeting to me. Mrs. Sneth didn't go on the field trip either. I won.

I had not heard anything from other schools. Maybe I sucked as a teacher and the word was out. The state of Washington was in a huge budget crisis. Millions of dollars were being cut from all types of funds. Few schools were advertising jobs early this year. So, I was faced with the reality that I might be back at the school the next year. Armed with that grim possibility I e-mailed Officer Lakewood after receiving a technology update from the district. They needed us to sign up for training during the summer of 2003. They needed to know what grade we were teaching in the fall. Perfect. It was an opportunity to ask her what was up on the front with deciding what grade I would teach. I e-mailed Officer Lakewood and said that I needed to know in order to fill out the forms. She asked me to schedule a meeting with her to discuss the possibilities. We met that afternoon. It was obvious ten seconds into our meeting that she had pulled out the "We don't know much" speech. She told me we didn't know enough yet to know who would be doing what next year. Numbers were still to be tallied for student count and teacher retirements. Numbers were still being crunched for building budgets, etc. She would keep me posted and let me know if there was an opportunity for next year. I was supposed to indicate that I would be teaching second grade on the form for the technology training. We could change it later if we needed to.

It was time for my end of the year evaluation. Officer Lakewood had been in my room four times that year. Two of them were formal observations. One time she came to collect some students for a project. The fourth visit was to ask me how I could make things work for Mrs. Craston after Curriculum Night. My evaluation was scheduled on a day that my spirits were low and my attitude raw. She started with a smile and asked, "How do you think things went this year, Joby?"

"This has been the most difficult year I have ever had teaching. This is a very restrictive environment. I have never worked in a school with as many outrageous rules and procedures as here. My creativity has been put on hold this entire year. There have not been any situations academically that I have had to think for myself. The curriculum is so prescriptive that there is no room for personal strengths to be applied. I am finding that if I am not like the other second grade teachers, some parents complain. This is the most difficult group of parents I have ever worked with. It is frustrating to work in a school where we never tell parents no."

Then it was silent. It had all poured out of me like poison. I told her what I really thought. With each statement I gained momentum and anger. It was scary. She sat there and looked dumbfounded. This was a different look from her normal "I disapprove" stare.

"Well, we certainly don't want anyone to feel that way. We take a team approach here on Mercer Island. We don't tell parents "no". We help them work with us to make sure everyone is satisfied. What can I do to help you?"

I thought about saying something like, "Run far away please". I held myself back and went on to say,

"You know, it has been a very long time since you have been the new person somewhere. You have been the principal here sixteen or so years. You have obviously forgotten what it is like to be new. The pressure here is intense. It is not a "safe" place to work. You constantly have to watch your step. The support safety network is not in place here."

"I don't believe many people feel that way."

"You are wrong. There are many people who are tired and feel the same way. Nobody has the guts or the energy to talk to you about it, except a few people."

As I envisioned my termination papers being drawn up, she apologized for it being a rough year, then wanted to talk more about the possibility of my teaching first grade or Kindergarten. Was it still true that I wanted to move to one of those grades? Yes it was. She said she would fill out the paperwork for the evaluation and put it in my mailbox. If I had questions, to ask, but that I had passed, no problem. I walked out of her office in a daze. It felt good to tell her what I thought finally, and to not just bitch about it behind her back. I figured any hope of getting out of second grade was blown up during the evaluation.

That afternoon I saw our school psychologist, Deb. She and I had exchanged thoughts about Officer Lakewood briefly earlier in the year. She agreed it was a restrictive environment. I told her what I had said to Lakewood and her only response was, "No shit!" I had earned her seal of approval. I could tell by the smile on her face. We were united on this front.

A few days later a white construction paper folder was in my mailbox with a huge red stamp on it "CONFIDENTIAL". This was it. This was the reckoning day. She was right. I had passed. I read the evaluation over. I was glad to see that she had made a mistake. She failed to add to the Professional Responsibilities section that I had served as the Technology Lead for second grade. So, I quickly slapped a sticky note on it telling her that she needed to add that before I could sign it. There was a lot of revenge in that. She did and I signed it.

Teacher Appreciation Week arrived. What an outpouring of appreciation there was. Darrin's mom arrived Monday morning of the week with a huge basket. She said I would need this, but didn't tell me what for. Each day the kids brought in gifts. Monday they all brought hand made cards and letters. Tuesday they each brought some kind of chocolate and put it in the basket. Wednesday they brought flowers. Room eleven smelled like a funeral home. Thursday they brought gifts. There were gift certificates to book stores, Starbucks, and more. There were books to read, candles, and the list went on. I was appreciated. What I have learned as a teacher is that typically when a parent doesn't say anything to you at all that you are appreciated. Some do make the effort to communicate their appreciations. I focus on the negative communication and let it discredit those who do appreciate my work. I received an e-mail from Kevin's mom and dad raving about how happy they were that Kevin was in my class, how it was a good match and how Kevin enjoyed it so. Ken's dad wrote me often and expressed his thanks for the hard work. Darrin's mother would pen me a note from time to time expressing her appreciation for the hard work. There were others too. Natalie's mother and father were grateful for how much she had grown in the area of responsibility and appreciated my high expectations in the area of Natalie being on task and getting work done on time. Not all of Mercer Island was crazy.

## MAY 2003

Stacy, Kim, Mary and I all signed up as the Volunteer Tea coordinators. The Volunteer Tea was a special tea to honor all of the volunteers who had given time to the school to help improve student learning. There was comfort in knowing that the four of us would whip that tea together and bare the burden together. On Mercer Island there was a specific way of doing things. Kim

TEACHING ON POVERTY ROCK

obtained the file from previous years on how things were done for the said tea. Some years cheesecake was served. Other years, fancy pastries and coffee were the spread. We all agreed that simplicity was the key to honor our school volunteers.

I was in charge of whipping up a magnificent invitation. We would send five hundred invitations home, one with each child to ensure we had covered every possible volunteer known to us. After all five hundred had been copied and distributed it was brought to my attention that I had misspelled a word on the invitation. We all agreed that we should not tell Officer Lakewood or she would surely come unglued. Nobody seemed to notice, or at least I never heard about it if they did. I figure the word was out about McGowan being fragile and a time bomb waiting to explode.

Kim kept Officer Lakewood abreast of all the ideas we had and plans that we made. The time was nearing and we needed to finalize the plans. We had changed the time of the tea from mid afternoon to the hour before school dismissed. The thinking behind this was so that parents could take their children with them when the tea was over and head home. Otherwise we feared there would be surprise visitors in classrooms from mothers and fathers who had an hour or so to kill before the school day came to a close. Officer Lakewood was unhappy with this change. "It has never been a problem in the past."

We had talked about giving each volunteer a lottery ticket with the theme of "Thanks a Million". Guess who shot that idea down? Tension was high and I resented that there was so much free advice from former volunteer committee members, Officer Lakewood, and whoever else thought they should throw in their opinion. I vowed never to be part of the volunteer tea again.

Officer Lakewood had passed out huge packets titled "The Final Five". These were checklists of everything that we needed to complete as teachers during the final five weeks of school. Five weeks felt like such a long time. The list had pages of items to tend to. Cum files were to be updated. Report cards had to be done. Addresses had to be updated in the office. Every chair, table, piece of equipment had to be counted in each classroom. The list went on and on. I began to plow into the list slowly over the next few days.

Giraffe Club Projects were due May 12th. On the morning of May 12th I received two e-mails from separate parents. One e-mail asked for an extension on the project because their child was so busy they didn't have time to complete it. The other e-mail said their child would not be completing the project for the same reason, lack of time. Now, I find it interesting when we are part of a community that demands higher standards and a higher work ethic that all of a sudden when the bar is raised we helicopter in to rescue our kids from assignments they have had six weeks to complete. In all, eleven out of twenty-three students completed a Giraffe Club Project. Nobody else bothered to do one. I made a huge to-do over the projects that were completed. I awarded certificates to those who met the goal and completed their project on time. I launched into a speech about responsibility, or lack there of. I explained how disappointing it was to have less than half of the class do the assignment. It made me think that maybe a portion of this population wanted higher expectations and higher workloads, but not if it meant they had to lend a hand at home to help out.

The projects that were completed were impressive. Darrin washed his parent's cars inside and out to earn money to buy school supplies for kids who couldn't afford their own in the greater Seattle area. Maya cleaned a local park and took pictures of the project. She and her dad walked to the park every day to collect trash. There was a picture of Maya holding two huge garbage bags full of debris. Eve had colored Easter Eggs and delivered them to a retirement home in the area. Those who completed the projects beamed as they presented. I truly was proud to say I was the teacher of these youngsters.

The week before the Giraffe Club projects were due I remember having a headlock with Jim. Jim had a passion for aircraft like none I had ever seen before. He knew every possible type of aircraft that ever existed, especially military aircraft. He had gone to great lengths to research aircraft types, draw and write about them. He continually blew me away with his knowledge of flight. Jim had talked Mrs. Keptog, our librarian, into allowing him to bring all kinds of model airplanes to the media center to set up a display for the school. For several days before the Giraffe Club Project due date Jim talked about how he had to race home after school to do more research about aircraft fighter jets and prepare materials for the library display. Each day he carted in more and more aircraft paraphernalia. The library was becoming a shrine to Jim's love for aircraft. I asked Jim if he had his Giraffe Club project finished mid-week. He told me no and that he wasn't going to be doing one. I asked why and he explained that his mother told him they were too busy and didn't have time. This was the exact attitude that floored me time and time again. We will do it if it works out with our schedule and if we feel like. I expressed my concern that he had spent each night preparing his aircraft materials for the library display, which was not an assignment, instead of working on the Giraffe Club Project. Jim shrugged his shoulders. He never did complete a Giraffe Club Project.

# JUNE 2003

I was impressed with how my kids in room eleven had grown

as authors. We had explored so many different types of writing from persuasive paragraphs to writing non-fiction autobiographies. Some kids wrote math autobiographies highlighting all the mathematical aspects of their own lives. It was like a transformation had occurred in these kids. They were eager and hungry to write alone and with partners. Several had churned out chapter books. We were publishing books on the computer and thoroughly charged by the writing spirit.

We agreed that we would have an Author Reading to celebrate our work as authors. I whipped up flyers telling the parents they were invited to come to the Author Reading. Each student would read something they wrote or a portion of a chapter book they had written. I asked the librarian if we could borrow her microphone and speakers. As a librarian and lover of books she was all for it.

Our class practiced on June 10ᵗʰ by inviting the other second grade classes to our room to listen to our Author Readings. Children read their work into the microphone. It was a tremendously positive experience for these kids. I beamed with pride. The Author Reading for parents was June 11ᵗʰ. On the morning of June 11ᵗʰ my e-mail was full. I clicked on an e-mail from Autumn's dad. He requested that she be excused from the Author Reading because it would be too hard for her and that she was too nervous to be in front of the class and parents to read. She didn't have any trouble having vocal confrontations with me in front of the class or lying and saying that I was kissing a student. I wrote him back and said I had every confidence in the world that she would do fine. I explained that she did an outstanding job the day prior on our trial run with other second grade classes. She smiled from ear to ear after she finished the day before. Still, he didn't want her to be forced to do this. What I found out was that Autumn wasn't forced to do much of anything. It really only ended up being a disservice to Autumn. Her name was already in the program and I wasn't going to redo them because she didn't want to be part of the Author Reading. Other kids asked her why she didn't read after it was over. I figured I would let her and dad explain that one.

For as much as this group of parents had expressed concern about the lack of opportunities to come to school and be a part of room eleven, I was sure we would have a full house. Eleven parents turned out.

I received an e-mail from Officer Lakewood asking me to meet with her about my plans for the following school year. I waltzed up to her holding cell that afternoon for the said meeting. The conversation went like this,

"Are you still thinking that you would like to move to Kindergarten or first grade next year?"

"Yes."

"Given the amount of concern you have had working with this population are you sure you are ready to handle parents of younger students? The younger the students, the more their parents are involved."

"Yes."

"I think there is the potential for you to be successful in first grade. But, I will have to check with the first grade team to see if they would be comfortable working with you next year and if they believe it is a good fit for them."

"OK."

"Please don't tell anyone about the possible move until I have talked with the first grade team."

"OK."

I walked out of her dungeon with a clearer sense of what she thought of me as a teacher. It was relatively apparent that her confidence in me was at an all time low. I had been in touch with every member of the first grade team prior to this meeting. They all assured me they would be glad to work with me. Officer Lakewood announced at the next staff meeting that I would be teaching first grade the following year. I overstepped my boundaries again and asked the members of the first grade team if in fact Officer Lakewood had checked with them to see if they thought I was a good fit or the team. She hadn't asked any of them what they thought of the plan. Officer Lakewood had a new title. It was "Micromanager Manipulator". The manipulator was added to enhance her already ever-present micromanaging.

Each class threw an end of the year party. My class was going to take a trip to the Bellevue Aquatic Center in Bellevue, Washington. It was just a few miles from Mercer Island. Arrangements were made. Notices were sent home and preparations were well underway. A few days later, Samantha's mom phoned to let me know there had been a scheduling error at the Bellevue Aquatic Center and we could no longer take the trip on the day we had planned. In a panic I sent an e-mail to the parents to let them know of the mishap and that an alternate plan was in the works. I would let them know as soon as we had something else lined up. Within minutes I had an e-mail from Kevin's mom, Tami. Kevin's mom and dad were members at the Mercerwood Shore Club, a fancy swimming and health club on Mercer Island. She called and they had availability for the original date we had scheduled the trip. I wrote her back and asked her to please book it. It seemed as though it would work out fine.

The day before the Mercerwood Shore Club party I got a call from Darrin's mom. Apparently Mrs. Craston was gravely concerned about the threat of rain on the day of the party. Mercerwood Shore Club had an outdoor pool. She thought we should look into alternate plans. So, she got Darrin's mom to research other options. Whatever havoc she could create by sidestepping contact with me seemed to be in order and on the top of her agenda. All the permission slips had already been sent home a week earlier. Children were assigned to a parent volunteer who would drive them to the event. If we changed the plan now at this last minute it meant we would have to phone each and every parent to inform them of the change and get verbal confirmation that they approved of us driving their children to a different location that we originally planned. My blood pressure rose. I needed some candy and a Pepsi to work through this one. Darrin's mom graciously called every parent that afternoon to inform him or her of the possible change. She confided in me that she had no problem with the kids swimming in the rain. There was rarely lightening in Seattle. I agreed. The kids would love to swim in the rain. The pool was heated. I called her up and said to forget it. We were going to Mercerwood rain or shine. She was relieved and glad that we saw it the same way. Reluctantly I told her that if there was any backlash from Mouth Craston to direct her to me. I would take all the heat from her.

The kids had a fantastic time. I was impressed and riveted by how many of them jumped off of the high dive. It was a great party. Again, I was humbled as they room parents pulled the kids together for cake and a pop. Samantha's mom gave a speech about how much they appreciated my work this year. I was handed a gift certificate to a local shopping center. All the students had donated money to get the gift.

The year was nearing an end. We had two weeks to wrap up the curriculum delivery and close the school year. I received an e-mail from Noor's dad.

"Hi Joby, Thank you for being gracious with Noor's birthday today. She was very pleased." I had allowed Noor to bring her birthday snack on a day where we had a zillion scheduling conflicts already. Yes, I did like it when parents realized that I granted permission for such events on a limited basis and when they were responsive enough to thank me. Maybe I had more of a hunger for power than I realized. The e-mail continued, "As the school year comes to an end we would like to thank you for making second grade a grand year for Noor. Thanks for communicating effectively, showing individual concern for Noor, and being consistent. Most of all, thank you for teaching Noor. The impact is long lasting. The respect and love for you will long be remembered. All the best for the upcoming summer."

As I sent the twenty-three second grade students, who were assigned to my leadership, home on the last day of school, I remembered thinking, "Look how far you have come." I was referring to myself. I had endured perhaps some of the most intense parental and administrative confrontation. As I turned in my "Final Five" packet with each responsibility signed and checked off indicating their completion, I smiled at Lee, our school secretary. I walked proudly from the school building. I clicked the unlock button for my car and threw my school bag into the backseat. I turned on the motor of my blue Volvo, put the car in gear, and sped up the hill and out of the parking lot to a summer of freedom that awaited me. Though I knew I would be back that fall, it didn't much seem to matter. I knew that somehow the following year would be better. For an instant I thought maybe I should read the S.O.P. manual before fall. With further thought I reminded myself that I had lived one entire year teaching on Poverty Rock without having done so. Year two was bound to be as exhilarating as the first.

# AFTERWORD

We ended up with a fantastic replacement for Mrs. Lakewood my second year at the school. I look forward to the great things that will happen under our new administrator's leadership. I am a much stronger teacher for having lived through my first year teaching on Poverty Rock

Printed in the United States
17428LVS00001B/4-66

9 781413 714555